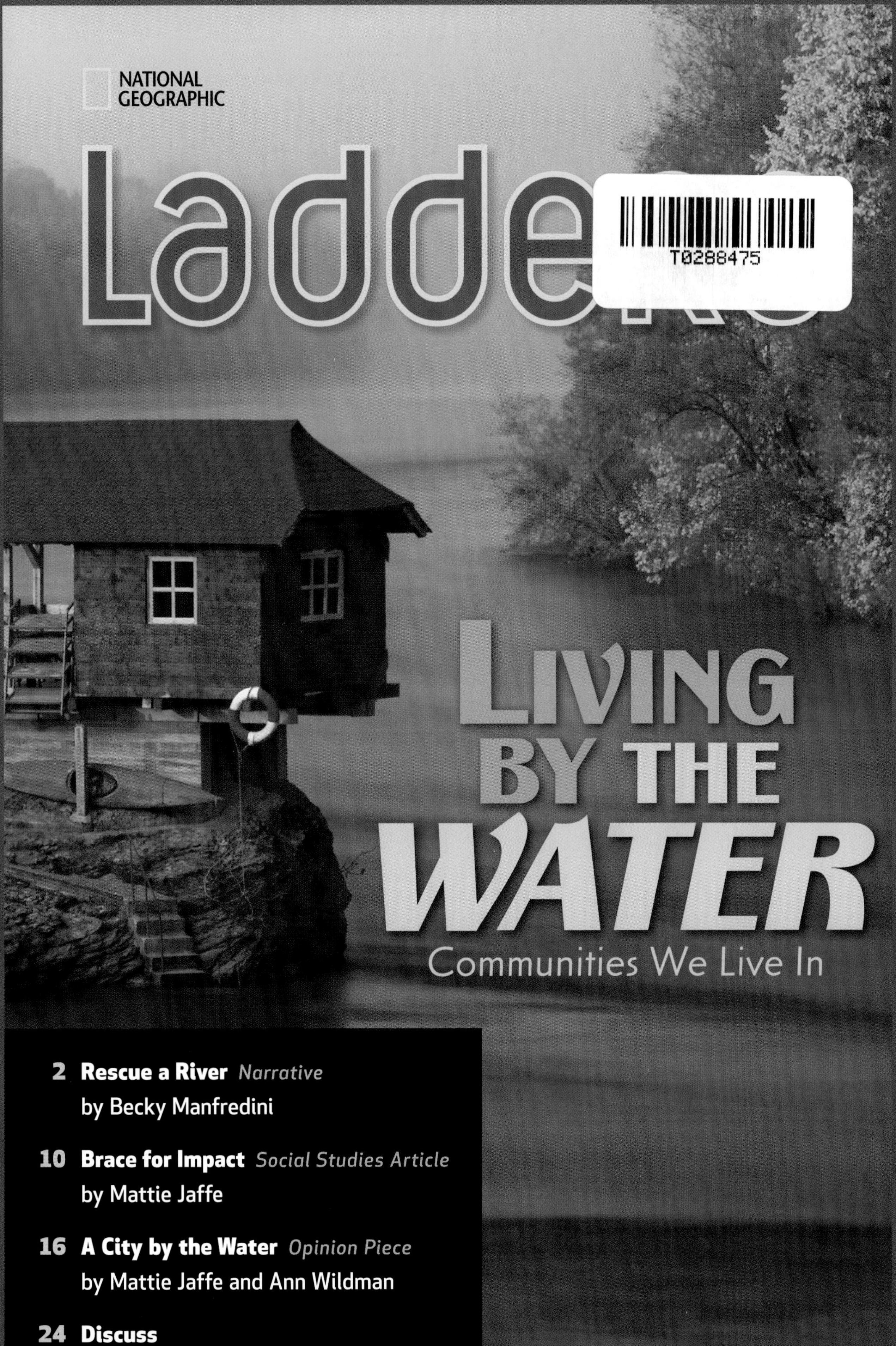

NATIONAL GEOGRAPHIC

Ladders

Living by the Water

Communities We Live In

GENRE Narrative

Read to find out about the Colorado River.

RESCUE A RIVER

by Becky Manfredini

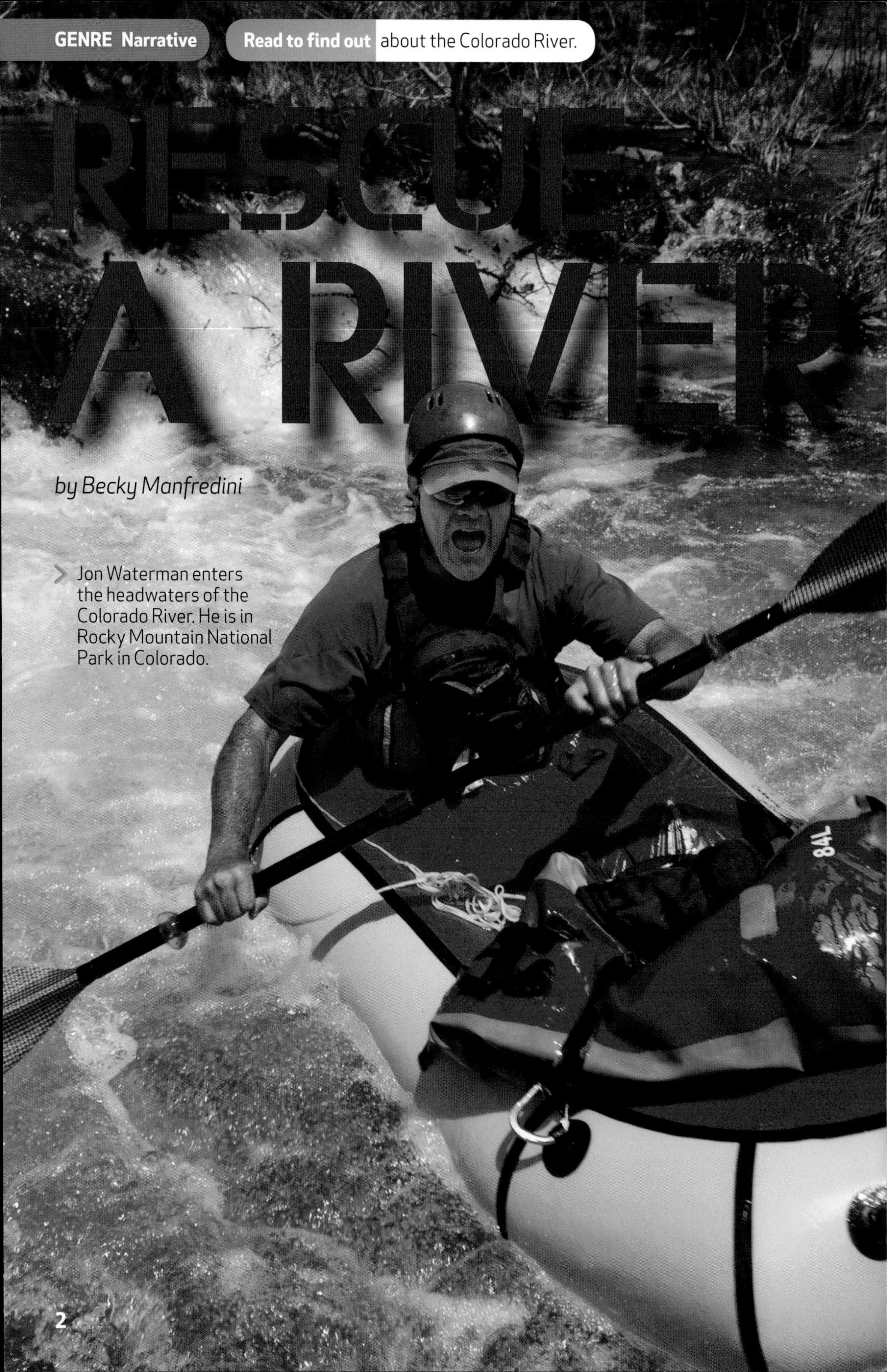

Jon Waterman enters the headwaters of the Colorado River. He is in Rocky Mountain National Park in Colorado.

Jon Waterman and Pete McBride are writers and photographers. One day in 2008, they packed their rafts for a long journey down the Colorado River. The men slid their rafts into the river high in the Rocky Mountains of Colorado. They were at the **headwaters**, or the beginning, of the river. Jon and Pete knew farms and communities in the region were using most of the river's water. They wanted to learn firsthand how this was affecting the river and those who depend on its water.

Jon would spend 150 days paddling 1,450 miles. Pete would join Jon for parts of the journey. Together they would explore the white-water rapids and cool, calm waters. But Pete would also photograph the Colorado River from a plane. He wanted to see what the river looked like from above.

Jon and Pete saw many different types of land on their trip. They saw the bright city of Las Vegas, the high cliffs of the Grand Canyon, and the deserts of northern Mexico. But the land wasn't the only thing that changed as the men paddled down the Colorado River. The river itself changed.

Jon Waterman travels around the world. He writes about the ways people can protect our planet.

Pete McBride uses a special camera when he takes photographs from a raft. His cameras are sealed so that water cannot leak inside them.

THE MIGHTY COLORADO RIVER

For six million years, the Colorado River flowed swiftly through the western United States and Mexico. Plants and fish filled its waters. But as the population grew in the southwestern United States, more people began using the mighty river's water. Today, more than 30 million people depend on the Colorado River for drinking, showering, and many other reasons. However, most of the river's water—78 percent—is being used by farms. As far away as California, water is being pumped from the Colorado River to grow various crops.

Jon checks out smaller rivers that flow into the Colorado River. This is the Rio Hardy. The word *rio* means river in Spanish.

As Jon and Pete explored the Colorado River in 2008, they noticed signs of the river's dropping water level. In fact, the Colorado River has dropped about 130 feet since 2000. That means less water is flowing through this river. Today, scientists worry that droughts—periods of low or no rainfall—and higher temperatures will continue to reduce the river's flow. Given how many people depend on this water source, what does this mean for the future?

THE COLORADO RIVER

A DISAPPEARING RIVER

When Jon and Pete reached the country of Mexico, the once-clear water they had paddled through turned into thick mud. It was so thick that their rafts became stuck. There was not enough water to move the rafts along. The men had to push their way out of the mud using their paddles.

The men wondered if this muddy mess would reach all the way to the river's delta. A **delta** is a region of land built by the sand and silt the river has carried to the sea. Until 1998, the Colorado River ended in a grassy delta as it flowed into the Gulf of California. The delta was filled with colorful birds and other wildlife. Today, it is less than 10 percent of its original size because the river has become

polluted and no longer flows to the Gulf of California. Sludgy mud has replaced its grass and flowing water. The land is now unsuitable for some animals, so they have wandered elsewhere for food and water.

The farther Jon and Pete traveled, the drier the river became. Eventually, they had to stop. The river had completely disappeared. They carried their rafts over their heads or on their backs. As the men looked around, they couldn't help but worry. While more than 300,000 birds stop along the river delta each year, resting here on their way to warmer places, their future is uncertain if the river and its delta are not restored to a healthier state.

^ In Mexico, the once-clear water of the Colorado River is now muddy and filled with trash.

WHAT COMMUNITIES CAN DO

One reason Jon and Pete made this journey was to show how important the Colorado River is to the animals in the region. The men want farms and cities to **conserve**, or protect, the river by using less water to grow crops and water lawns and keeping the river clean and flowing. Then plants and animals won't lose their homes. Together, they are writing books and making films to spread the message: Save the Colorado River!

Jon and Pete's journey down the Colorado River teaches us that rivers are important to our future. They carry **fresh water** to the communities that need it. Fresh water contains little salt, unlike the salty water in the ocean. We grow our food with it, drink fresh water, and wash with it. We need to make sure it is clean and plentiful.

Jon carries his belongings on his back. He is walking across a dry stretch where the Colorado River used to flow to get to a place where the river is still flowing.

CONSERVE OUR PLANET'S FRESH WATER

Conserve water at home. Limit the use of tap water for showers and brushing your teeth. Use plants in your lawn that don't need a lot of water. And only water your lawn early or late in the day.

Pick up litter around rivers and lakes. Polluted water harms animals. Polluted water can't be used by communities.

Turn off lights when they're not in use. Power plants use water to create electricity. If you use less electricity, power plants can make less electricity and use less water.

Eat less meat. Farms use water to grow crops that feed animals being raised as food. Animals also need to drink water. If you eat less meat, fewer animals will be raised as food. Less water will be necessary to raise them.

Check In Explain what is happening to the water in the Colorado River. Why does the river need to be saved?

GENRE **Social Studies Article**

Read to find out how different members of a river community worked together in an emergency.

Brace for

IT WAS THE AFTERNOON OF JANUARY 15, 2009.

The 155 passengers and crew members aboard U.S. Airways Flight 1549 fastened their seat belts. At 3:25 p.m., the plane took off from New York's LaGuardia Airport. It was headed to Charlotte, North Carolina.

Less than two minutes after the plane left the ground, passenger Eric Stevenson peered out the window next to his seat on the plane and noticed a flock of geese flying next to the aircraft. Seconds later he heard some loud thuds and smelled something burning.

At the same time in the cockpit, Captain Chesley "Sully" Sullenberger and his copilot Jeff Skiles were thinking quickly. The plane had flown through a flock of Canada geese. Some of the birds had been struck and had jammed the engines. The plane had lost power.

Passengers make their way onto the plane's wings. They wait to be rescued from the middle of New York's Hudson River.

IMPACT

by Mattie Jaffe

Skiles went through a checklist of actions to restart the engines, but nothing worked. There was no time to return to the airport or to fly to another one. Captain Sullenberger would have to make an emergency landing. But where? Then he saw a wide, open space below them—the Hudson River. It was dangerous, but landing on the water close to a big community was their only choice.

Captain Sullenberger made a calm announcement on the loudspeaker: "Brace for impact." Passengers prepared themselves for an emergency landing. They leaned forward and placed their feet flat on the floor.

Captain Sullenberger fell in love with flying and airplanes when he was a boy growing up in the state of Texas. He became a pilot in the United States Air Force. During his 30-year career, Sully's top priority was always safety. As a former flight instructor, he taught others how to fly safely. After the event on the Hudson River, Sully began working with the Young Eagles, a group that teaches children about airplanes.

A MIRACLE ON THE HUDSON

Less than six short minutes after taking off from LaGuardia airport, the huge plane dropped onto the Hudson River in New York City.

Sully was a very experienced pilot. He knew to ease the plane slowly onto the water. He didn't want the plane to flip when it hit the water. He also didn't want to land too slowly and crash the plane nose-first into the Hudson. Sully landed the plane perfectly. The quick thinking of Sully and his crew saved everyone on board the plane.

Emergency workers put on scuba gear so they can dive into the freezing water.

Firefighters throw a rope to passengers. The rope is used to secure the raft.

Landing the plane on the water also protected the people of New York City—a community on the water—from being hurt. New York City is packed tight with buildings and people. If the plane had gone down on the ground, many more people's lives could have been in danger.

As soon as the plane hit the Hudson, the **waterway** sprang to life. The Coast Guard and other rescue workers spotted passengers waiting on the plane's wings. Boats sped away from their piers to come help the passengers. **Ferryboats**, which normally carry people back and forth across the Hudson River, raced toward the plane to transport the aircraft's passengers to safety. The passengers could see that New Yorkers would rescue them quickly. They were soaked and freezing, but they were alive!

Rescuers help passengers get into a raft near the tail of the jet.

COMING TOGETHER

Once the plane's passengers had been safely taken aboard the rescue boats, workers gave the freezing survivors warm clothing. The boats brought the plane's passengers to shore.

Then the people on land stepped up to help out. Local restaurants welcomed passengers. Servers gave them food, warm drinks—even the clothes off their backs. Nurses and

Many different types of boats help in the rescue.

doctors at local hospitals cared for passengers who had been hurt in the water landing. The New York City community came together and showed the passengers of Flight 1549 how much they cared.

Many people, including Michael Bloomberg, the mayor of New York City, praised Captain Sullenberger. They called him a hero for his calm, skillful emergency landing on the water. However, Sully praised his crew. "I was very happy that everyone involved did their jobs extraordinarily well."

Check In What caused the plane to crash?

GENRE Opinion Piece **Read to find out** about the pros and cons of living in New Orleans.

A City by

by Mattie Jaffe and Ann Wildman

Just Call Me "NOLA."

Listen closely and you'll catch the lively sound of a trumpet blasting a tune in the distance. Breathe in the smell of fresh seafood gumbo as it wafts past your nose. Watch a 100-year-old riverboat churn the water as it lazily passes by on the Mississippi River. You're in New Orleans, Louisiana, or "NOLA," as people fondly call this city on the water.

New Orleans is almost surrounded by water. The city is located along the Mississippi River. Several lakes and the Gulf of Mexico are also nearby. This city's location has made it an important **port** since the 1700s. A port is a place on the water where ships load and unload goods. Around 6,000 ships travel along the Mississippi each year.

the Water

A look at New Orleans from across the Mississippi River

They bring boxes of goods in and out of New Orleans, and all of this shipping gives many people jobs to do.

When they aren't working, the people of New Orleans have fun along the water. But summers in New Orleans can be very hot and steamy. Hurricanes, or storms with strong winds that occur over warm ocean waters, sometimes threaten the city during the fall. New Orleans can be a stormy place to live!

The French Quarter is a very old neighborhood in New Orleans. It is known for its historic buildings.

A Stormy City

In August 2005, weather forecasters tracked a growing hurricane in the Gulf of Mexico. Would it hit New Orleans? On August 29, it did. The strength of Hurricane Katrina caught many people by surprise. Within hours, cars looked like submarines under rising floodwaters. Trees were flattened. Houses were destroyed. Hundreds of thousands of people had no electricity.

What caused all of this damage? Strong winds up to 170 miles-per-hour caused Gulf waters to rise. Eventually, the water spilled over the **levee** walls. Levees were built around New Orleans to protect it from flooding. Everyone knew that flooding was a risk in this low-lying city so close to the water, but they thought the levees would help. Unfortunately, Katrina was just too powerful.

> Hurricane Katrina caused 80 percent of New Orleans to flood.

Once the storm passed, groups, such as the American Red Cross, that help people in need, provided shelters and hot meals. They also gave families clothing and groceries. Volunteers built safe homes for people whose homes were destroyed by Hurricane Katrina.

It took several years, but New Orleans became a thriving city again, and visitors returned to enjoy the activities that make New Orleans special. The levees were also strengthened to keep New Orleans safe in case another massive storm hits.

Hurricane Katrina was the largest hurricane to hit the United States.

A volunteer saws lumber. He is helping rebuild a home near New Orleans.

Down on the Bayou

When stormy weather isn't threatening New Orleans, people do things outside—such as visiting the **bayou** (BY-oo). Bayous are marshy, slow-moving streams. There are many bayous near New Orleans.

If you'd like to see the animals and plants of the bayou, then sign up for a swamp tour. You can hop aboard a regular boat for a calm and quiet ride. You can also take an airboat for a fast and noisy tour. Airboats are small boats with a large fan on the back. Steamy swamp air blasts through the fan to blow the boat across the water.

^ The bayous near New Orleans are home to many alligators.

v In the fall, some trees in the bayou turn orange.

Some of the first things you'll notice in the bayou are the soft strands of moss that seem to drip from the branches of the bayou's trees. These mossy trees have strong roots that grow together into a wall below the water. The root walls help block floodwaters from moving from rivers into cities such as New Orleans.

In the bayou, the bugs swarm around you like a thick cloud. There are plenty of animals to see, too. Alligators live in the bayous. So do egrets, which are large, beautiful wading birds. And don't miss the nutria, which look a little like beavers with long, rat-like tails. It's amazing that this wild setting is so close to the crowds and noises of the city of New Orleans.

Let Loose

Besides the swampy bayous, New Orleans is known for one of the liveliest parties in the country—Mardi Gras (MAHR-dee GRAH). This huge party happens before a long holiday of fasting, or not eating certain foods. Mardi Gras is a chance for large crowds to eat, be silly, and let loose.

Some of the best parts of Mardi Gras are the parades. People wear fancy handmade costumes and glittery masks. They hop on the floats and toss gifts such as beaded necklaces and plastic coins to the crowd. These gifts are called "throws." Kids dress up in funny costumes hoping to get more throws. Catch one if you can! Throws are good luck.

Anyone can join special Mardi Gras parades called "second line parades." They feature musicians playing **jazz**.

Jazz is a type of music that has a strong beat and features instruments such as horns, drums, and pianos. In a second line parade, the sounds of the horns and drums catch people's attention as the musicians move down the street. Parade watchers can join in the fun by dancing behind the musicians.

New Orleans' location near the water can bring storms and flooding. However, the jazz music, food, and celebrations of the city, along with the adventure found in the bayous, make living in New Orleans exciting.

^ People spend all year building floats. Floats are made of wood and plaster.

v Street bands lead dancers in a second line parade.

Check In Name one reason someone might want to live in New Orleans. Name one reason someone might not want to live there.

Discuss

1. What connects the three selections that you read in this book?
2. How do the communities along the Colorado River use the river's water? What are some ways communities such as yours can conserve water from rivers and lakes?
3. How did the water community of New York City work together to rescue the passengers of Flight 1549?
4. How does the location of New Orleans affect the people who live there?
5. What do you still wonder about living by the water?